IF THESE SCARS COULD TALK

WOMEN TRANSFORMING WOUNDS INTO WISDOM

Stories by Cassandra Cean-Owens, Chrystal Colón, Shameeka France, Kifana Longdon-Gordon, Jusinta Jaggassar-Ernul, K. Sweetness Jennings, Samantha J. Lawrence, Penelope Martin, Turquoise Juanita Martin, Sequoia Patterson, Helen "Skip" Skipper, Bridget Wilson

Compiled by Nadia Lopez, Ph. D. and Taiia Smart Young

DEDICATION

For the hundreds of thousands of women

and girls incarcerated around the world.

This is for the times they made you feel less than.

They didn't acknowledge your humanness.

They refused to listen to your story.

We've taken back our power and put it into words.

CONTENTS

Acknowledgements vii

Preface - *Dr. Nadia Lopez*.. viii

Joy Cometh in the Morning - *Cassandra Cean-Owens*............................ 1

Loss, Resilience, and the Cost of Redemption - *Chrystal Colón* 7

The Transformational Power of Pain - *Shameeka France*...................... 13

A House Divided: Fighting for Dignity, Family, and Legacy - *Jusinta Jaggassar-Ernul* 17

More Like a Rescue - *K. Sweetness Jennings* 23

Survival Mode - *Samantha J. Lawrence*... 29

Leaving the Crossfire - *Kifana Longdon-Gordon* 35

Make It Make Sense: How Long Do I Mourn? - *Penelope Martin* 39

Babyfa$e: From Takeover to Triumph - *Turquoise Juanita Martin*......... 45

Searching For Love - *Sequoia Patterson* 53

I Am the Change - *Helen "Skip" Skipper* 59

My Father Taught Me How to Be a Side Chick - *Bridget Wilson*......... 63

The Last Word - *Taiia Smart Young* 71

Meet the Authors 72

L to R: Dr. Nadia Lopez, Taiia Smart Young, and April Walker

ACKNOWLEDGEMENTS

This vision came to life thanks to the contributions of an incredible team. April Walker, iconic fashion designer, styled each woman in her renowned *Walker Wear* line with the assistance of Kyeisha Kelly. Danielle Henry, celebrity makeup artist, and her team worked tirelessly to bring out the unique beauty of each participant. And Barnabas Crosby, with the support of his team, Rudie Canty and Darrell Day, masterfully captured the essence of these women through his photographic lens. Their work brought artistry and dignity to this project, elevating it beyond words on a page to a powerful visual narrative.

I also want to extend my deepest thanks and gratitude to my CCF team, especially Nicole and Raquisha, for their unwavering commitment to seeing this project through. Their dedication and support have been instrumental in bringing this anthology to life. My heartfelt thanks also go to Sheryl Prince and her team at Noire Publishing House for their work in ensuring this anthology was published on time. Their dedication and professionalism have been invaluable in bringing this vision to fruition. This program is supported, in part, by public funds from the New York City Department of Cultural Affairs, in partnership with the City Council.

- **Dr. Nadia Lopez**, Chief Impact Officer, College and Community Fellowship

PREFACE

When the idea for *If These Scars Could Talk* first emerged, it was rooted in the desire to create a space for women who have been incarcerated to reclaim their voices. Too often, these women are silenced or shamed into not speaking about their journeys. They are mothers, wives, daughters, and sisters—human beings whose paths to incarceration were shaped by trauma, survival, grief, abuse, poverty, poor choices, and untreated mental health issues. Despite having served their time, they remain stigmatized by society. Yet, they persevere. They are resilient and hopeful, pursuing degrees, obtaining certifications, and navigating countless barriers to create lives filled with purpose and possibility.

This anthology is the outcome of L.I.T.T.Y (Literature Inspires, Teaches, and Transforms You), a program launched in October 2024 and facilitated by Taiia Smart Young. As we celebrate 25 years of College and Community Fellowship (CCF) supporting women in achieving higher education and certifications, we are reminded of the importance of amplifying the voices of our members, especially those who are formerly incarcerated. Over five months, these extraordinary women came together virtually through L.I.T.T.Y to share their stories and engage in the writing process with their coach. Each session revealed their courage and vulnerability, captivating all who listened. Initially, the goal was simple: to create an anthology that would allow their voices to live out in the world. But as their words flowed and connections deepened, it became clear that this project was about more than storytelling, it was about sisterhood. By mid-February, the virtual connections transformed into a profound in-person gathering. In a safe and welcoming space, these women shared laughter, tears, and stories that cemented their bond and celebrated their collective strength.

But capturing their words was not enough. It was essential to capture their images as well, to see them as they truly are—beyond the criminalized and dehumanizing photos so often associated with incarceration. A picture is worth a thousand words, yet for many formerly incarcerated individuals, their most publicized images are mugshots tied to moments of harm. This anthology celebrates their beauty, freedom, and power. Each woman is depicted in her full complexity and humanity, a reminder that they are worthy of being seen and celebrated.

It is my hope that this anthology shifts the narrative around justice-involved women. Through these pages, we must come to understand their stories, invest in their futures, and provide the respect and resources they deserve to thrive. May *If These Scars Could Talk* inspire you to see into the hearts of these remarkable women. Their stories are not just theirs; they are ours to honor, learn from, and uplift us.

- Dr. Nadia Lopez

JOY COMETH IN THE MORNING

———○———

Cassandra Cean-Owens

The doctor, sitting behind his desk, leaned in to explain the results of the examination he'd just performed. His words sounded more like a curse than a medical diagnosis. "You are a fibroid farm! Not even a champion sperm donor could get you pregnant." The doctor spat these words at me as if he were God and my body was nothing more than a defective field, a waste of space incapable of bearing children.

The doctor's words haunted me for years and the disappointment in his eyes still lingers in my mind today. For three years, he'd worked to rid me of my fibroids. Three months after my second surgery to remove them, they had started growing back. But I knew better than to let this steal my joy, and I rebuked each word of his curse in his heart.

I was 34, with five years of marriage under my belt and I'd never been pregnant. Friends offered me their thoughtful diagnoses: "You're too stressed," they said. Or, "You work too hard." Still, the years of barrenness stretched on. I worked hard, carried on and tried to silence the longing for motherhood. To others, I had everything: a wonderful husband, who was attentive, caring, loving, smart, tall, dark, handsome and kind; and I had a good life. And I did have a good life and a busy business, but inside, the feeling of emptiness remained.

The emptiness turned into confusion, pain and shame when I faced a new personal challenge in May 2011, a criminal charge. October 1st, 2013, I sat on a cold, hard bench outside of a courtroom with my husband beside me. I turned to him and said, "God just told me that today might be my worst birthday ever, but next year will be my best." I believed it. I clung to that whisper of hope as we entered the courtroom.

Although I wasn't knowingly guilty of committing fraud as an attorney, the judge didn't see naivety as an excuse. Less than seven days later, I was pronounced guilty of wire fraud and conspiracy to commit wire fraud. Still, I believed a blessing was headed my way. God had promised me one and I knew he wouldn't forsake me, not when I needed him the most. And, He could and would save me from this conviction and prison because: "What God can't do doesn't exist!"

As I waited for my sentencing date, I threw myself into prayer and fasting, pleading with God for a breakthrough. For three days, I ate nothing. I called it the Esther Fast. Then I continued for 15 days, avoiding meat and sugar, doubling down on vegetables, and I called this the Daniel Fast. I ended with another three days of complete fasting for a total of 21 days, surely, this would get God's attention.

On Sunday, the week before the final day of my fast, I sat in church as the pastor called for a blessing over the womb of women who were having difficulty conceiving. I rose to go forward, but a voice stopped me. "Sit down. You are already blessed." Shocked and bewildered, I quickly turned around, walked as fast as I could and sat back down. When the pastor called again, I stood up and began walking down the row of red cushioned brass chairs. And again, the voice spoke to me: "Did I not tell you to sit down? All you want is for people to pity you. Sit down," the voice insisted!

Days later, on the last day of the fast, I felt different. My body felt strange, my breasts were tender, my body heavy. Was I...? I got up and went to the pharmacy for a pregnancy test, and when I took it, two pink lines appeared on the plastic wand. My husband began screaming with uncontrollable joy: "You're pregnant!" For a moment, I thought, *How in the world does he know what these two pink lines mean?* But he was right. Indeed, I was pregnant!

But our family's joy was short-lived. My sentencing day had arrived, and I stood in court, four and a half months pregnant, as the judge handed down my fate: seven years and three months in prison. The prosecution painted my pregnancy as a deliberate ploy to evade punishment. The judge, a former prosecutor himself, sided with the prosecutor. He sentenced me to begin my prison term one month before my due date. This felt particularly cruel, especially since the judge knew I had a high-risk pregnancy.

My attorney, bewildered, asked if the judge had heard him when he mentioned that the baby could arrive in October or November. The judge barked, "If she is still pregnant in September when she is scheduled to surrender, then we'll revisit it."

This felt like a second curse pronounced over my womb. I trusted God, even though I knew this challenge ahead of me wasn't easy. When September rolled around my baby was still growing inside of my belly. Seeing this, the judge delayed my surrender date until after my daughter was born. Just as God had promised, my next birthday (my 40th) was the best one yet. That was the day my angel, my baby CassieAnn (short for Cassandra's Angel) was born.

In November 2015, I surrendered to begin my sentence. Walking through those prison doors, I carried the weight of a mother's heartbreak. Leaving my daughter behind felt like she was being pulled right out of my womb. Yet, still, I believed, maybe because there was nothing else that I could do. Every night, I wondered if Cassie missed me or if she would remember me.

Less than two years into my prison sentence, on June 1, 2017, I faced an even greater tragedy. The chaplain arrived with news of my father's death. My father's passing was sudden and it hit me hard because he was my voice of wisdom. He put incarceration into perspective for me, by challenging me to see it as a time to reflect on what I valued most, instead of seeing prison as a death sentence. And just as I was coming to terms with that loss, three months later, the chaplain came again, this time, my mother was gone.

My mother, who was non-verbal due to illness, never knew I was incarcerated. My father feared it was too much for her heart to handle. So, we kept this secret from her, but I know she felt my absence, and then my dad's absence. The weight of losing them both while confined behind bars was suffocating and cruel. But even in my brokenness, God was working on my behalf. Each crack in my heart, each fracture in my soul, was forming a testimony.

In prison, Cassie consumed my thoughts. I worried about her well-being, and wondered if she ever thought about me. A child psychologist visited us yearly in prison to prepare mothers for the inevitable question: "Where's Mommy?" The psychologist said children typically understand that their mothers aren't around by age six. The following year, she said five. Each year, the number shrank and my hope dimmed. Based on my paperwork, I wouldn't be released until Cassie was 7½ years old. But God would surprise me once more. I was released early from prison when she was 5 ½ years old.

When I was released in 2020, I did what so many told me not to do. I tried to make up for lost time with my daughter. Some advised me to let go of the guilt, but I couldn't. I immersed myself in Cassie's world. Helping her with homework and cuddling her to sleep with bedtime stories. Her favorite was *Charlie and the Chocolate Factory*. Every moment was precious. I was no longer an absentee mother from behind bars. I was present.

While I was incarcerated, my husband held our family together. His strength never wavered. He brought Cassie to visit me, made sure she knew I loved her, even if she couldn't feel my hugs every night. He navigated the challenges of raising a child while his wife was away. He was my anchor, my partner through the good, bad and terrible, and proved to be my greatest earthly blessing.

Redemption and true motherhood weren't just words for me they became my reality. I found purpose in the prayer line God led me to start two days after leaving prison and in my work at REFORM Alliance (REFORM), using my story to uplift others, just as their stories had uplifted me. Through praying for others on the prayer line and working at REFORM, God transformed suffering into my testimony.

Now, as the prayer line celebrates its fifth anniversary this year —To God Be the Glory— it has grown from meeting three days a week (Monday, Wednesday, and Friday at 7 AM EST) to gathering every single day, seven days a week at 7 AM EST. When I first came home from prison during COVID, the prayer line served as a space where others who had also been released joined me in praying for those still inside, asking for their safety and release. Today, it is not only a place for justice-impacted women to pray, praise, and worship God, but it has also become a powerful lifeline for professionals, some who have never even been to prison, who seek and offer prayer, upliftment, fellowship, and a life-changing experience every morning at 7 AM EST.

This is not just my story. It is the story of countless incarcerated women burdened by deprivation of motherhood, shame, loss and injustice. Yet, through it all, we discover a strength we never knew we had. We rise. We heal. We are redeemed. And through it all, His promises are kept, and we become blessed and refreshed.

LOSS, RESILIENCE, AND THE COST OF REDEMPTION

Chrystal Colón

I had plans of starting a new chapter in California. At the time my son, my first child, was just a month old. I was still breastfeeding, trying to balance being a new mom. But then, I got arrested, yet again, and everything changed.

My crimes were always about opportunity. If I saw something available, like a gym locker unlocked, I took the opportunity. I'd find handbags, with wallets and credit cards that I would take. But I always left everything else behind because, in my mind, those other items were personal. I rationalized my actions, convincing myself it wasn't really wrong because, after all, the banks were insured. The women could report the theft, and they'd get their money back in a few days. I even justified it by recalling times when I had to report my own lost cards. To me, it felt like a victimless crime.

I used to frequent this specific gym chain in NYC. There were approximately nine of them in Manhattan alone. Back in 2010, memberships cost over $100 a month. The gyms were filled with working professionals, and I thought if they could afford those memberships, they weren't struggling. I'd use the cards to buy necessities. But my reasoning was flawed, and deep down, I knew it. Over time, my actions caught up with me.

It's not that I didn't understand right from wrong. I just couldn't see the harm at the time. I came from a world where material things mattered, and survival often meant bending the rules. My mother had always taken care of us. She was a stay-at-home mom, supported by the trust fund my father left us when he passed. He worked for Metro North and ensured we'd have financial support after his death. My mom received $800 monthly for her four kids until we turned 18. She made sure we had everything we needed—the latest sneakers, clothes, you name it. She groomed us to present ourselves well, no matter what.

But everything changed when my mom passed away. I was just 15. She had always been our anchor. Even as she battled illness, she made us believe that God would heal her. We grew up in the church, and her faith was unshakable. She would say, "God will work a miracle." We believed her. Even as she wasted away, losing 30, 40, and 50 pounds, she held on to her faith. She stopped taking her medication, convinced it wasn't necessary. For a brief moment, she felt better, but it was too late. She was gone, just like that.

Losing her was devastating. My siblings and I weren't prepared. She had always shielded and kept us together; now, we were left to navigate life independently. My maternal grandmother stepped in, but it wasn't the same. She watched over us, but she wasn't strict or nurturing like my mom had been. I blamed her for a lot. As the matriarch, I felt she should have done more. But the truth is, she did the best she could with what she had.

After my mom's death, I threw myself into school and extracurriculars. I graduated high school on time, though my grades weren't the best. I was the captain of the dance team, involved in step, and stayed active to keep myself going. Of my siblings, I was the only one who managed to graduate on time. But when I turned 18, everything shifted again.

The trust fund my father left me was finally released, allowing me to live comfortably for a year. I attended college upstate, relishing the independence that financial security provided. But by 19, the money was gone. Suddenly, I had nothing. My grandmother couldn't support me financially, and I had no idea how to make ends meet. I just knew I needed to survive.

That's when the cracks started to show. I transferred to different colleges, trying to find my footing. I went to five schools in total, each time hoping for a fresh start. But without money, I couldn't stay in one place for long. At 19, I started working at Sketchers, my first real job. But even before that, I had already started taking shortcuts.

It began with small thefts. At first, they were just necessities: underwear, shirts, and pants. I started shoplifting from places like Macy's and Bloomingdale's. Eventually, I got caught. Back then, stores had holding cells in the back, which I now know were illegal. But it didn't stop me. By the time I was working at Sketchers, I had transitioned from shoplifting to stealing credit cards. It felt like a natural progression.

Looking back, I can see how my upbringing influenced my actions. Growing up, my mom had always made sure we had the best. When I lost that security, I didn't know how to cope. I wanted to maintain the image I had grown up with, but I didn't have the means to do it legitimately.

I've had time to reflect on my choices. My father's death, my mother's illness, and the loss of stability all played a role in shaping who I became. My dad passed away when I was six, and for years, we were told it was a stroke. But when I was around ten, my mom sat us down and told us the truth. He had died from AIDS. She explained that she had contracted HIV from him and was also living with the disease. That conversation changed everything.

I remember the stigma, the fear. One time, I cut my hand playing baseball. It was a deep wound, and my mom was hesitant to help me clean it. She was afraid of transmitting the virus to me, even though it wasn't possible in that situation. Moments like that stuck with me. They showed me how much she was struggling, not just physically but emotionally.

My mother was young when she died—34 years old. She had been a force of nature, but she was also human. She made mistakes, and she had her flaws. But she loved us fiercely and did everything possible to give us a good life. Losing her left a void that I didn't know how to fill.

For years, I carried anger and resentment. I was angry at her for not preparing us for her death, for making us believe she would be okay. I was angry at my grandmother for not stepping up how I thought she should have. And I was angry at myself for not being stronger.

As I grew older, I began to understand the complexity of my experiences. My life of crime wasn't just about greed or materialism. It was about survival, about trying to find a way to navigate a world that felt overwhelming and unforgiving. I made mistakes, and I've paid for them. But those mistakes don't define me.

Today, I'm working on rebuilding my life. I've come to terms with my past and the scars it's left behind. Those scars tell a story of resilience, of learning to rise above circumstances that could have broken me. They remind me of where I've been and how far I've come.

If these scars could talk, they'd tell you about a young girl who lost her parents too soon and struggled to find her way in a world that often felt cold, judgmental, and unkind. They'd tell you about the mistakes she made and the lessons she learned. And they'd tell you about the woman she's becoming—stronger, wiser, and determined to transform her wounds into wisdom.

THE TRANSFORMATIONAL POWER OF PAIN

Shameeka France

My journey to freedom was anything but ordinary. After serving time in Federal Satellite Low in Danbury, Connecticut and Camp Cupcake in West Virginia, I was released into a world that had been changed by the pandemic of 2020. The streets were empty, stores sold bleach at triple the price and refrigerated trucks sat outside hospitals with rows of deceased bodies.

Everyone seemed to be involved in Paycheck Protection Program or PPP loans for short, whether they had a small business or not. Bitcoin was available on the stock market, but not long ago, it was a tool for black-market purchases.

I came home to a world full of darkness. Standing on Guy Brewer and Farmers Boulevard in Queens, I watched as people gambled on the corner. Among them was an artist (I won't name names) who said to me, "Ya Highness, let's go one more time. We're not eating. We're chewing right now." They were gambling with $10,000 on the dirty concrete. I lifted my pants leg, showing the ankle monitor on my right leg. They handed me $2,000, and then praised me for surviving the feds. It was surreal.

I made it home in time for my daughter's 10th birthday. We celebrated with a penthouse party, something I never thought I'd be able to give her. For one beautiful night, surrounded by family and friends, I felt blessed. In that moment, I felt free. But despite the chaos around me, I stayed on course.

Fraud was rampant, people were making and blowing money fast, but I wasn't going back. After being offered 120 months (plus five years) I served only 48 months, my mission was simple: never return.

There were some people who helped me turn my life around. I was fortunate to be accepted into Justice Through Code (JTC) at Columbia University. I owe a huge thank-you to Aiden McDonald for ensuring people like me understood the importance of technology. Alongside my fellow "queens" and "kings" of code, I learned Django, Python and data analysis. Technology became my beacon, propelling me into a future I'd only dreamed of. Susan, an attorney at Columbia University, who was also the CEO of the Broadway Advocacy Coalition convinced me to see a play focused on prison life, but none of the cast had been incarcerated. That bothered me, but during this play, there was a moment of silence for the late Kathy Boudin, whose post-justice involved work paved the way for people like me.

Working for the Women's Prison Association (WPA) was another blessing. Thomas Phillips, who hired me as a community worker. I distributed HIV test kits, Narcan and fentanyl test strips across the five boroughs. During the pandemic, while the world stood still, I was on the move, determined to save lives. Through the Collective Leadership Institute (CLI) at Columbia, I connected with women worldwide, all dedicated to social justice. Together, we addressed how the justice system impacts Black and Brown communities. I also worked to place 100 families into permanent housing in New York. My journey expanded from local to national advocacy through organizations like the National Council for Incarcerated and Formerly Incarcerated Women and Girls. Andrea James and Grandma Phyllis Harding became my guiding lights.

On the other hand, my personal challenges loomed large. During my incarceration, my daughter endured trauma, including sexual assault, which crushed me. I faced the consequences of my absence and navigated a world where the new norms often felt alien. Despite this, I remained steadfast, praying and working to heal both myself and my child. In 2024, I was diagnosed with multiple sclerosis (MS). What I initially thought was lingering pain from a 2021 car accident turned out to be something far more significant. The diagnosis felt like a death sentence. But now, in March 2025, I've learned to embrace my journey. MS is part of my story, but it doesn't define me.

To commemorate five years of freedom, I've contributed to this anthology as a testament to my resilience. Impossible isn't a word in my vocabulary, instead, I see it as "I'm possible." This book represents light in a dark place, a reminder to stay the course no matter what. My journey has been shaped by countless individuals who believed in me. From Judge May, who saw my potential, to my sister Josie, who pulled me from darkness, and even those who failed me, each one played a role. I owe them a debt of gratitude.

I've dedicated my life to ensuring the next generation of leaders doesn't need to navigate darkness to find their light. Whether it was organizing free community events, providing school supplies or simply showing up for someone in need, I've aimed to create a legacy of giving back. I've turned pain into passion and passion into power. I'm focused because of the pain I've experienced, and for that, I'm grateful.

A HOUSE DIVIDED: FIGHTING FOR DIGNITY, FAMILY, AND LEGACY

Jusinta Jaggassar-Ernul

I called 911, hysterical. "It's an emergency! Please dispatch the fire department—my elder and disabled parents are inside the house and not responding."

In less than 20 minutes, the NYC Fire Department arrived. The fireman knocked on the door, but there was no answer. I explained that I had just received a call from our family in Trinidad & Tobago informing me that my aunt had passed away. My father's family had also tried reaching him but couldn't get in touch with him or my mother. The fireman quickly responded and used an ax to open the door. Upon the loud pounding of the ax, I heard my mother's faint voice: "I'm here." We entered and found my father on the floor, my mother pale and weak, and the house in a state of disrepair—no heat, no hot water, unpaid bills, and untouched medications. Despite my parents' protests that they were "fine," it was clear this was a medical, mental and maternal health emergency.

My father, a hard working immigrant from the West Indies, had spent decades working two jobs to provide for his family. My mother juggled her job with raising her children, community children and extended relatives. Yet now, lying in front of me, they were vulnerable, and their home—a symbol of their sacrifices—had a "For Sale" sign lying near the garbage can.

17

A Daughter's Fight for Her Parents' Future

Their stories didn't add up. This wasn't just about their declining health; it was about their retirement investments and future stability. My parents, like so many elders, faced daily battles: managing bills, maintaining the house, managing multiple medications, scheduling multiple doctor appointments, and the uncertainty of their retirement. Yet, their biggest fear was losing their independence.

I had seen too many elders stripped of their dignity, forced into institutional care because they lacked living trusts, wills, healthcare proxies, advanced health care directives or a support system. Families left unprepared—children unequipped to take over responsibilities—often led to crises like this. I knew I had to act fast. Adult Protective Services called, informing me that my parents needed housing. After 28 years as homeowners, their home was being sold by my eldest brother and sister, who claimed ownership but offered no support in helping them downsize. Instead, she dragged them through court, immorally accessed an early inheritance, and spread malicious rumors about my parents and anyone who tried to help.

With no remorse, she attempted to commit my father to a nursing home, falsely accused me of mental instability, and even tried to place my children in foster care. She disappeared with their life savings, leaving both my parents and their siblings in financial ruin.

Breaking Cycles of Harm and Building Legacy

Hurt and betrayed, I sought legal help. My incarceration has taught me the importance of having proper legal representation, access to community resources and being informed to navigate systems that are not designed for the marginalized to succeed. I worked tirelessly, determined to protect my parents and my children. A healthcare broker, Ms. Rose English became a guiding light, sharing resources to secure long-term home care services for my parents—services I, too, would one day want for myself.

Through this ordeal, I realized this wasn't just about my parents. It was about families like ours—the "sandwich generation"—caught between caring for aging parents and raising children.

My struggles taught me that access to elder care, parenting rights, and support healthcare/human services can make all the difference. Families don't just need homes; they need wraparound services that address financial trauma, medical, emotional, and social needs. Aging in place gracefully shouldn't be a privilege. It shouldn't become a police matter nor lead to family court prosecution, tearing families apart. Instead, it should be an accessible, dignified choice.

Families need **community-integrated healthcare** to manage chronic illnesses, mental health, financial healing and daily wellness. **Long-term home care assistance** for daily tasks while preserving autonomy, safety and independence. **Reliable transportation services** to prevent isolation and to ensure dignity care. **Emotional and social support** to combat loneliness, fraud, and mistreatment. I advocate for these things—not just for my parents, but for my children, my community, and myself. Stability, health, safety and dignity aren't just about survival; they're about respect, autonomy, cultural connection, and equitable access to shared resources.

Caring for my parents as they navigate multiple chronic illnesses has brought my journey full circle. I thank my silent partner (BAE) for being my rock and my best friend. There was a time when my parents taught me to save money and prepared me for life. And there were times when I, too, needed someone to advocate for me. Now, it's my turn. Rehabilitation & Recovery Advocacy is about breaking cycles of harm, building intergenerational support, and ensuring that no elder parent nor caretaker fights alone. It's about creating a world where families can age in place, parents and children are supported and surrounded by love and care, with access to higher standards of living, improved quality of life, culturally informed, trauma-sensitive and anti-violence services.

Alternatives to nursing homes and alternative to foster care systems of care exist, but we must dismantle barriers to systemic health inequities, end racially discriminatory policies, remove predatory wealth building, increase harm reduction communal care, invest in peer mental health/substance use resources; including community health workers, access to credible messengers, access higher standards of legal education, prevention and protections for disabled, marginalized and vulnerable families, children, parents, grandparents and intergenerational person centered communities.

To God Be the Glory,
Proverbs 31 Woman

MORE LIKE A RESCUE

─────○─────

K. Sweetness Jennings

Shall I let a simple profound idea shift my way of thinking into some different divine, deep, three-dimensional mantra to replace when I doubt myself. Shall I stand in the truth of the creator's definition of me? Shall I walk in confidence, and be my best self, no matter what? Shall I sit with grace and allow mercy to comfort me? If only I could while sitting behind a door without a knob.

The reality of the matter is I kept making mistake after mistake. I gave birth at 15, just two months shy of my 16th birthday. In 1977, I was categorized as an unwed mother. It took me 12 years to get married and when I did, this man knew little about being a husband to a hurt, misunderstood and insecure young girl. I made a strong attempt to be what others wanted me to be, but I failed at every turn, which left me sitting behind a door without a doorknob at 30, more than 31 years ago.

My next mistake was using and abusing drugs, which led me down a dark and frightening path. Shame and guilt were my constant companions during that season of my eventful life. The drug use left me in debt. I owed a drug dealer money, and his solution was for me to deliver a package to his friend in another country. For years, I asked myself why I agreed to such an outrageous suggestion. After arriving in a country I was unfamiliar with, I was told by the man who sent me to go to a hotel and wait for a phone call. However, fate had other plans. I was arrested at the airport. In retrospect, it was a rescue more than an arrest. I never made it to the hotel. A male and female police officer asked me to come with them for a search. They led me to a room about 12 by 14 feet with two large desks and a few chairs.

The woman officer said, "We will be conducting a cavity search. Do you know what that means?"

"No, I do not understand what you're talking about," I said. Fear overwhelmed me. "What seems to be the problem?"

The officer answered, "We have reason to believe you are carrying drugs into our country. You can cooperate, or we will forcibly remove your pants for the search. The choice is yours."

Panic set in. Slowly, I pulled my pants down. When they reached my knees, I was told to bend over. I did as instructed, the officer removed the package from between my legs. Embarrassment, shame, fear and anger consumed me in that moment. After the drugs were confiscated, I was taken to the police station to be charged and booked.

One day, I sat on the edge of the bed, getting dressed for court. I put on the dark suit, the white blouse, and the modest hairstyle we wear to give the impression we are "nice ladies worthy of a second chance." I wanted to scream, "I am not that person on the piece of paper accused of importing a controlled substance with intent to sell!" That paper did not tell my story. I am a wife and a mother of two beautiful sons with promising futures. I'm a human being who made a life-altering mistake.

If I could speak things into existence, I would declare: "I am a woman pushing past obstacles, no matter what. I am a diamond in the making. I am a college graduate, a poet and a substance abuse counselor. Don't my clothes tell you these truths?" But my saga didn't begin at that airport. No, it started with the abandonment I felt as a child, immediately after my father left when I was just a kid. Imagine, if you can, an underdeveloped mind, given limited views of life, formed by half-truths and misguided perspectives. That was what directed my thinking. The perfect storm of self-doubt, fear, and loneliness eventually took me to places I didn't want to go, doing things I knew were wrong.

The shame from this event flows through me as freely as my own blood. I committed a felony crime. That label brought its own trauma and internal scars. My motherhood was challenged and my position as a wife was questioned. When a father leaves, failing to protect and affirm his daughter, many things are bound to happen. My father left me standardless.

Who looks at the soul of another? Who does that?

Some scars are soul-deep.

At 12, I felt abandoned by my father. My parents fought often in front of my siblings and me. You'd think I'd felt relieved when he left, but I wasn't. Before he left, he was kind to me. He'd hug me and buy me dolls and toys. His absence created a void, one I tried to fill with unsavory men who were always older. At the time, the attention from these older men felt good. But I stayed afraid. Lonely and afraid—a dangerous combination. If my scars could talk, they'd tell you: "She doesn't look like what she's been through." The scars qualify me as a warrior. They're not always visible, but they're there— woven into my relationships, my family dynamics and my health. The emotional scars stem largely from the disconnect with my father. Growing up without his love and protection filled me with anger, fear and insecurity. Behind that door with no doorknob, I asked myself over and over, "How did I get here?"

The anger was deadly most days. It manifested into piercing stares and harsh words. It stemmed from my fear of not being enough or not being lovable. The emotional scars took a physical toll: bags under my eyes, weight gain, poor posture, high blood pressure and borderline diabetes. It even interfered with my ability to breathe deeply and digest food properly.

The shame of leaving my sons, embarrassing my family and stepping outside my marriage haunted me. In retrospect, how could I not use drugs? How could I not cheat on my husband? How could I not put drugs in my underwear? Lost, confused, and insecure I made choices that led to incarceration. The spiritual scars of doubt and low self-esteem hindered me from really liking myself. The doorknob was intentionally missing. Behind that door, I had time to think, reflect and heal. I began to believe in forgiveness—first from God, then from myself. Source (the God of my understanding) sent people to guide me: mentors, pastors and a dean who helped me see my potential. I graduated college and pursued a career as a substance abuse counselor, using my past as a stepping stone toward helping others. The best is still yet to come.

IN CLOSING, A NOTE TO MYSELF:

Look at you Katherine René Farrington Sweetness Jennings. Look at you paying attention long enough to hear the voice and touch of the God of your understanding. Allowing the Process to work in your favor and believing beyond seeing.

Look at you thriving despite it all. You've turned trauma into triumph, shame into strength and pain into purpose. Prayer changes people and it changes things.

I like how you get back up after falling so many times. I enjoy watching you release the shame and guilt of past mistakes, making room for increase beyond your wildest dreams. Past mistakes shall not define you.

You have the audacity to use your trauma as a stepping stone toward your goals. Watching you over the years reach beyond what you know and obtaining what you thought wasn't possible. You are living proof that abundance is here, within you and around you. You've inspired others and shown them what grace looks like.

Thank you for allowing your words to create your world.

THE WIND IS BENEATH MY WINGS AND SOARING WITH THE EAGLES IS MY DESTINY.

SURVIVAL MODE

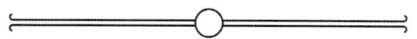

Samantha J. Lawrence

It all started on the block of Whitman Junior High School. If you were a fly girl, you were in a crew. And if you were in a crew, you rocked Sergio Valentino jeans and early-release Jordans with confidence. And if you were in a crew, you had to be ready to fight.

The East Flatbush Fly Girls had their way of making a name for themselves. It wasn't just about style; it was about survival. In the streets, your reputation mattered and there were Crips, Bloods and get-fly high schoolers watching from the sidelines, waiting to see who would rise and who would fall.

"TRS ain't nothing to fuck with!" we cheered, our voices bouncing off the third-floor staircase in school. It was a warning to the Life crew. The message was clear: Meet us at 3 p.m., outside. No backing down.

That day should have been like any other. But when the crowd gathered, the air was thick with something different. I stood, fists clenched, as the voices rose around me. "Beat her ass!"the crowd shouted, pushing me forward.

Keisha stood in front of me, stance ready. Jays laced up. A Polo sweater hugged her chest, Girbaud jeans were tight around her hips and a full, sew-in bang swayed as she stepped forward. My crew greased my face and slipped a ring onto my finger. A steel-coated promise of victory.

My first hit was electric. The ring sliced her cheek, and as her blood trickled down her face, I felt a rush of something could've easily been mistaken for power. Bama, Keisha's boyfriend—a Blood—watched from the crowd, and his expression let me know he was mad at her.

Keisha ran home. I followed her, even though I was suddenly afraid of what would happen next. When Keisha returned, she'd changed into something more appropriate for a fight. This time, it was Timbs, a wife beater and a head tie. Her mother stood behind her, and the fight resumed. But I won. Again. And for that, she was beaten—by her mother and later, by Bama.

Not too long after the fight, Liberty, Keisha's cousin, came up to me in school, looking uneasy, her eyes darting around as she spoke.

"Yo, Samantha, we need to talk," Liberty said.

I frowned. Liberty wasn't the type to seek me out. "What's up?"

"Bama wanna see you."

My stomach twisted. "For what?"

Liberty shrugged, looking past me and lowering her voice a bit. "I don't know. But he said he wanna see you after school. Told me to tell you."

I hesitated, my heart hammering inside my chest. Bama wasn't just some high school boy. He was 19 and he wasn't just a Blood, he was a Blood general. If he called for you, you didn't ask why—you showed up.

"Where?" I asked, my voice lowered to match Liberty's.

"His people's crib. They be chillin' over on 31st Street."

I clenched my fists at my sides, trying to act like this was nothing. "Aight."

"You sure?" Liberty paused. You don't gotta go, Sam."

I forced a smirk, ignoring the pit in my stomach. "Nah, it's cool. I have to walk pass to go home. It's whatever."

She nodded slowly, like she wasn't convinced. "Aight. Be safe."

As I watched Liberty walk away, the air around me felt heavier. I should've paid attention to that pit in my stomach. I should've said, "No." But instead, I showed up. I took my naïve, 13-year-old self to meet a guy who was six years older than me.

At 19, Bama was a man. I didn't know it then, but he would be the first to show me how power and violence would be used for control and to create fear. Bama sat on the edge of the bed, cornrows slicked back, clear beads clicking as he looked up at me. His red bandana was tied tight around his head and his presence sucked all of the air out of the room.

"Samantha," he said, his deep Caribbean accent made my name sound different, kinda tropical. "Take my pager and dial 411. So I know it's you. I want you to come over to my house tomorrow."

I nodded. "Okay," I said softly. I had never been to a boy's house before.

Girlhood, Interrupted

The next day, I went to his house. My stomach was in knots. My palms were damp. The room smelled like cologne, sweat, something else I couldn't place.

"Samantha, lie on the bed," Bama said.

I froze. "For what?"

"Have you had sex before?" he asked, ignoring my question.

"No."

"So, you're a virgin?" he said, looking directly into my eyes.

"Yes." My voice shook.

He nodded like he was deciding something. "I want you to be my girl. And if you want to be my girl, you have to have sex with me."

There was a pit in my stomach again. "I'm scared. I-I-I don't want to."

He exhaled sharply, eyes darkening. "I can call someone else who wants to be with me here."

I swallowed hard as he pulled off his wife beater. "Take off your clothes," he said. "And lie down."

I didn't move. If I didn't listen to Bama, he could get another girl to replace me. But if I stayed…I'd be someone. I'd be Bama's girl. That title came with respect. It made the recipient untouchable. I stood there, staring at the floor, not sure of what came next. Bama knew exactly what to do. His arms were long. He walked over to me and placed my hands on his chest. My hands looked so small against his skin. Bama grabbed a towel and placed it on the bunk bed. I thought I was going to pee on myself as he pulled off my jeans. I wanted to stop him, but I was scared. It all happened so fast, one minute I'm fully clothed and the next he's on top pressing down on me. His weight made it hard for me to breathe. My body was stiff, frozen. I tried to scream, but the sound wouldn't come out. My throat felt like it was closing as my mind searched for a way out of this mess.

"You think you're tough?" he sneered, grabbing my wrist. "All that fighting, but you ain't got no fight left now, do you?"

"Let me go, Bama," I whispered, barely audible.

"Nah," he laughed, tightening his grip. His weight suffocated me. "You mine now." His cousins and his friends, my classmates, were there. They heard. They saw. And they did nothing. I thought I was going to die as the veins bulge from his neck. I cursed myself for stepping inside his house, for believing I was safe.

So many thoughts collided in my head. Maybe if I went along with it, it wouldn't hurt as much. Maybe if I pretended to like it, it would be over faster. Don't resist. Don't make him angry. Don't cry. This is what I told myself. I closed my eyes and let it happen. The room was silent except for Bama's breathing. Heavy. Deep. Satisfied.

When it was over, my body was sore and my skin felt dirty. I wasn't the same. I stared at the ceiling, wishing I could disappear, wishing I could undo everything. But most of all, I wished I'd never spoken to Liberty that day, never heard Bama's name, never walked into this room. But it was too late. The damage was done.

Girls Like Me

This was the first time I learned two valuable lessons. First, to some men, I was nothing more than a body to be used and second, the world doesn't save girls like me. So, I stopped expecting to be rescued and learned to save myself. Honestly, my spirituality saved me. When the weight of my past threatened to pull me under, when suicidal thoughts whispered that I was nothing more than used goods, it was my faith that anchored me. I attempted to end it all four times, believing the world had no space for me, that I had been too broken, too discarded. But something greater than me refused to let me go. Through prayer, searching and reconnecting with a power beyond this world, I found the strength to keep living. My faith did not erase my past but it gave me a path forward. This story is mine, but it is not just for me. It is for every girl who has been ignored, blamed or silenced. For every survivor still searching for their voice, you are not alone. And if the world refuses to listen, tell your story anyway.

LEAVING THE CROSSFIRE

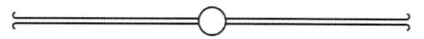

Kifana Longdon-Gordon

The tapestry of my life is a vibrant, chaotic and an undeniably unique creation. At 42, I stand in the middle of the threads of motherhood and a past that, while I wouldn't wish to relive, has undeniably woven its way into the woman I am today. Mine is a history with four sons and a history marked by both deep love and regrettable choices. It's a story that could fill volumes, but here, I'll try to capture its essence.

My eldest son, now almost a man at 24 years old, entered my world when I was barely a woman, just 16. The whirlwind of young motherhood swept me away. It was a mix of overwhelming love and the stark reality of responsibility. My parents, bless their hearts, stepped in to fill the gaps in my fledgling maturity. They provided a safety net, a haven of support that allowed me to finish high school. Looking back, I see their generosity, but at the time, it felt different. I craved independence, and the ability to provide for my son the way they provided for me. It was a noble aspiration, twisted by the naivete of youth and a desperate desire to prove myself.

That desire, unfortunately, led me down a dark path. My best friend, who worked at the local restaurant after school, inadvertently introduced me to the world of credit card fraud. In those days, receipts displayed the full card information, which was a vulnerability my friend exploited. She'd bring home discarded receipts, and together, we'd embark on online shopping sprees. It started innocently enough—

baby clothes, things my son "needed." But the thrill of easy money, the ability to acquire what I thought I lacked, quickly became addictive.

The skills I learned in those early days, skills I'm deeply ashamed of now, only became more refined and more sophisticated as time went on. My life became a cycle of highs and lows, and the adrenaline rush of illicit activity followed by the inevitable crash of consequences. Arrests. Court dates. Fear of being caught. Getting caught. It was a self-made prison, and my two oldest sons, now 24 and 16, were caught in the crossfire. The guilt I carry for the time I missed with them and the instability they experienced, is a weight I bear every single day. I can never fully erase the past, but I strive to build a better future for them and myself.

A Flicker of Hope

Later, I had twins. At the time, I was still entangled in the web of my past mistakes. Even though I was trying to distance myself from that life, my hands weren't clean. The charges from 2015 resurfaced, and I found myself facing the consequences of my actions while three months pregnant with my youngest boys. It was a devastating blow, a stark reminder that the past doesn't simply disappear. But amidst the fear and despair, a flicker of hope ignited. The twins became my catalyst for change. I knew, with every fiber of my being, that I could not continue down the dangerous path I was on. I had to break the cycle, not just for myself, but for my sons, all of them.

That realization propelled me forward. I earned my degree in Business Administration with a focus in Human Resources, a testament to my determination to build a legitimate and fulfilling career. I became a tax preparer, an honest skill I use to provide for my family. I'm pursuing further education to become a Human Service Professional. This path resonates deeply with me, a chance to give back to my community and help others who may be struggling, just as I once did.

The journey hasn't been easy. There are days when the guilt threatens to consume me when the memories of my mistakes haunt my dreams. But I refuse to let the past define me. I am a mother, a professional, a survivor. I am a work in progress, constantly striving to be a better version of myself. My story is not one of redemption, because redemption is a gift I don't feel I deserve. It's a story of resilience, the power of love, and the unwavering belief in the possibility of change. It's a story that's still being written, and I pray that the remaining chapters will be filled with more joy than sorrow, more light than darkness. It's a story that reminds me, every single day, that even from the ashes of our mistakes, we can rise and create a life worth living.

MAKE IT MAKE SENSE: HOW LONG DO I MOURN?

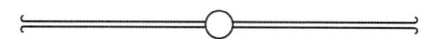

Penelope Martin

Mourning begins...

Feelings of pure joy, shadowed by gut-wrenching sorrow.

For Amanda, life begins

Sadly, for Frankie Mae life comes to an end

My firstborn, Amanda, will sleep in her own crib tonight,

While I cry myself to sleep missing one of the most important people in my life.

Was my daughter born to carry Frankie Mae's spirit?

Is Amanda destined for greatness?

Her first night in her home,

Full of love and light

It is not so vibrant today.

My emotions are all over, not knowing if I should be sad around my child,

I do not want her to feel this type of pain and heartache.

Mourning is so complicated.

Frankie Mae watches over me,

This I know.

She has given me strength on numerous occasions

To endure this roller coaster called life.

She is *still* my rock.

I feel like I have failed her on so many levels.

Failures that might not have occurred if I could still hear her voice,

A vivacious voice I can no longer remember.

A voice that could have saved me from

Not being able to raise my children

Becoming a drug addict

Going to prison

For taking a life

Mourning is underrated...

When can I let go of the uncertainties that embody this old relationship?

Will I ever recover the parts of me

Lost with Frankie Mae's passing?

Probably not,

Those parts were shed to create space

For all the new parts of myself

I am still discovering.

Discovering sobriety

Discovering responsibility

Discovering the importance of education

And discovering, I must love me first

It's complicated…

But I let go of my fears

Faced them head on,

Instead of avoiding them through drugs and alcohol.

I could do no wrong in Frankie Mae's eyes.

She always found a way to show me how I could do better without criticism.

Memories flood my mind often

And yet Frankie Mae is faceless in them all.

Mourning is complicated...

Sadness creeps in whenever I reflect

On the summers spent in her Georgia home.

A home so welcoming and inviting

No one was ever turned away.

The floral patterns on the wallpaper were unique to her.

The carpeting felt like velvet under your feet.

And all the aroma when she was cooking.

I experienced a plethora of emotions when Frankie left me.

Yes, I definitely feel abandoned by Frankie Mae.

Through no fault of her own.

That is my own selfish need for her unconditional love.

A love that can never be duplicated or replaced.

Mourning never ends...

Her delicate, yet strong face is fading.

I don't see traces of her anywhere anymore.

How long is too long

To mourn the most influential person

You've had in your life?

In loving memory of my dear grandmother Franky Mae and beautiful angel Amanda.

BABYFA$E: FROM TAKEOVER TO TRIUMPH

—————◯—————

Turquoise Juanita Martin

One night, my uncle tried to kill me, he placed a plastic bag over my head and I had to fight my way out of it. This was after years of being in foster care–people thought he cared about me,but his home was a mindfield. I was always in survival mode. I ended up in a series of foster homes. Ultimately I was placed in a group home and eventually went AWOL, so I had no other choice but to figure out my life–really quick. By then, school was not my priority, I made the choice to drop out. I tried to stay with my mom after she cleaned up from drug addiction, but we realized our relationship was better built on different terms–just not under the same roof. The place I could finally land safely was at Big Sis's house, she was a neighbor, I would babysit her kids for free and she would do my hair occasionally. It was where I could find a little bit of peace in the midst of all the chaos.

Big Sis had a connect at a strip club in Jersey, and I was down to shake what my mama gave me to earn some extra cash. The fast food was wack. Working at McDonald's for minimum wage wasn't it, not when I had already made $50 a day in cash as a look out. But staying up all night with no real place to sleep was another kind of wack. I needed a new plan.

The Game Chose Me

It was a gorgeous, sunny day when I met Rich. My bodysuit and jeans offered the right amount of warmth as I trooped uptown to The Hill to see my people. I needed some weed to ease my mind and my period cramps. I'd barely made it ten blocks when I locked eyes with a tall, licorice-painted dude copping socks from a street vendor.

He mouthed, "Hello," and I caught a glimpse of his pearly whites and feline features. I returned his greeting with a low whisper and kept it pushing.

"Yo, Ma!" he yelled to regain my attention.

I smirked and kept walking, but his voice had a lil' thing to it, a smooth, intoxicating command.

His footsteps hit the concrete in a rhythmic beat as he tried to catch up with me. "The only reason I'm calling you Ma is because I don't know your name," he said. "I'm Rich."

His eyes traced my face, breasts and finally, my hip to waist ratio. I could practically see him making quick calculations. Rich said he had a girl named, Chyna Whyte, who made money at parties but he didn't like her working solo. He thought I'd be a perfect addition to the team. Then, he said something about weed. Now, Rich had my attention.

As we walked to his house, Rich told me how happy Chyna would be to meet me. We entered this building on 119th Street, and I walked behind him into the huge apartment. He went to wake Chyna from her nap. When Rich returned, he rolled up and we took turns hitting the blunt.

"Have you ever danced before?" he said, after blowing a thick cloud of smoke in the air.

I followed and blew out my cloud. "I love to dance."

"Yeah, but have you ever danced *on stage?*"

"At talent shows." That was my response. I was so green.

Chyna appeared in the doorway. She was golden from her tresses to the glow of her skin. I was in awe of her nonchalance and confidence—the only thing she wore was a smile. Rich didn't need to do anymore convincing. I was down.

Chyna grabbed an outfit for me to try on, before returning to her nap. Rich turned on some music and asked me to dance. I was a bit self-conscious, but I obliged him, and I blushed when he called me sexy. It wasn't my first time hearing that, but blushing felt like the polite thing to do. Then, he schooled me about what went down at these parties. There was more than just dancing. VIPs were either a lap dance, blow job or going all the way. He insisted that I use condoms and said it was my job to "beat the clock" and make a dude bust in ten minutes or the length of two songs.

Before I knew it, Rich had me practicing with a condom on him. "You beat the clock, bitch!" he said, smiling. I should've been offended but I wasn't. I had already passed my first test. That night, I learned how to "stuff" for my period, got my makeup done, and was introduced to my new identity.

"You're 22, studying psychology and dancing to pay for school," Chyna told me.

"Is Rich coming back? I asked, as she applied liner to my eyelid.

"We'll meet him outside. But don't ever call him by his name, especially in the spots or around other players. We call him, Poppa."

I listened, not fully sure what she meant, but certain I would soon find out.

Chyna continued, "You in the game now, baby. We don't look other pimps in their face. Don't worry, I'll point them out to you. Put your head down and stay in pocket. If you dance in front of a guy and he doesn't tip you, turn around and pull ya G-string a lil, if he still don't tip you, move on to the next guy. If you dancing with a guy and he's tipping, stay there."

I tried to process all of this new information.

"If he's consistent with the money, lean over and ask if he wants a lap dance. Lap dances are $20 a song, if he wants you to dance for another song, it's another $20. Poppa told you about VIPs?

"Uh huh."

"Good. Make sure they give you the money first. Take it to Poppa and then you go do the VIP. Also don't forget to clean up when they tip you, guys tend not to tip you if they see you got a lot of dollars on you. And them hating hoes might try to snatch your dollars. So, just find Poppa and clean up every now and then throughout the night." Chyna was 363 days older than me and had the wisdom of a vet. "Did Poppa give you a name?" she said, digging in her bag for a hairbrush.

I shook my head from side to side as we went outside to meet Poppa. He held a cab door open for us. In the backseat, Rich broke out in excitement, about how much money I was going to make that night, how the first night was always special and how we were going to be a family now.

"Do you have butterflies?" Poppa asked.

I most certainly did and I told him so.

He responded with sheer excitement, "God, I miss that feeling!"

I smiled, wondering if I would ever be as poised as Chyna or as sure of myself as Poppa.

Then came the stage name. "Babyface!" Chyna blurted out, grinning.

"What's that?" I said, amused and confused.

"Your stage name!" she replied. Poppa agreed that it fit me.

I smiled. It was settled. My new name was Babyface. And that's who I became.

The Renegade Rises

When my moms got sick, Poppa sent me to be with her. "You gotta keep your head on straight out here, that's why we don't drink and smoke while we work," he said. "Can't have you worrying about moms on that floor. When she gets better, you can come back home."

She didn't get better though. She transitioned and, in a way, I did too. I didn't go back home. Other pimps would've kept me in their stable just for bragging rights, but this time I was on my own. I'd officially turned 22, had my first kid, and was working as a renegade, a sex worker who takes care of themselves without a pimp. I was indoctrinated by the best. Rich was my pimp and I never had another. Besides, I was already spoiled. Rich had been good to me. He worked it out with my mom so I could continue to get my GED, stack a trade and see her every Sunday for dinner. I was in the game but I wasn't lost. Rich kept my hair, nails and fit right, and a roof over my head.

The Fall: Rock Bottom

Drinking, drugs and constant partying blurred the lines of reality. Addiction crept into my life as both an escape and necessity. It numbed the pain, masked the trauma and kept me functioning in a world where survival depended on me playing a role. The game, with its pimp, players and the underground hustle, became my reality. It promised protection and security, but in truth it took more than it ever gave.

Losing my son to child services shattered me in ways I didn't know was possible. I was drowning in the life that took everything from me and I didn't know how to fight for a better one.

At my lowest, I overdosed on Ecstasy. I wanted a way out and taking those ten pills seemed to be the solution. But I woke up. I felt a presence, a power in the room and knew this was my last chance to change my life. Change didn't come easy. The streets had its grip on me and without a plan, without support, the pull of the old life felt stronger than the dream of something better.

The Fight: Rebuilding From the Ashes

The game hardened me but it didn't break me. It taught me resilience, adaptability and survival. It gave me a name when the world tried to erase me. But I was more than Babyface. I was a mother. A woman. A survivor. And my story was far from over. Getting clean wasn't just about putting the drugs down. It was about confronting the pain I had been running from. Healing the wounds under the addiction was a battle. I sought therapy, joined support groups, tended to my spiritual condition and surrounded myself with people who saw potential rather than my past.

Those special people told me the war was over. Slowly, I began to surrender. Eventually the weight of the abuse I endured, the trauma, the streets, the loss, guilt and shame began to lift. And I was tired of carrying it. The biggest challenge was proving to myself that I was worthy of being a mother to my son. I had repeated the generational mistake of allowing others to care for my son. My uncle fought me for custody of my son and the system had written me off as another statistic. I refused to lose my son to the system or the streets. I had a parent advocate through the Bronx Defenders, who helped me to navigate the system. With their help, I learned how to advocate for myself and my child. I attended every meeting, every court date, every parenting class. I had to show them (and myself) that I was capable of being the mother my son deserved, that generational curses could be broken.

I began rebuilding my future. I enrolled in college, won scholarships, obtained two degrees, and completed certifications. Education became my redemption, proof that I was not defined by my past but by my ability to rise above it. The same system that once deemed me unfit to be a parent is now the field others navigate. My son's high school awarded me a Parent Leadership Award. And my son, the brightest thing in my sky, is my biggest motivation, supporter and inspiration.

Trauma to Healing

Now, I stand on the other side of my darkest days. I secured housing and got my son back on Valentine's Day 2014. I kept a roof over our heads and my promise to stay clean. My degrees have opened doors I never thought was possible, giving me the tools to create a future I once believed was out of reach.

But most importantly, I reclaimed my power. No longer bound by addiction or the streets, I now use my experiences to uplift others through my public speaking and business ventures incorporating spiritual empowerment and personal advocacy into my mission of teaching radical, magical, self care to my community.

I understand what it's like to feel lost, to believe that change is impossible. But I also know the power of transformation. I am living proof that no matter how dark or deep the pit, there is always a way out.

For anyone who feels trapped, who believes there is no way out, let my journey be a testament: you can rise. You can rebuild. And you can reclaim your life.

SEARCHING FOR LOVE

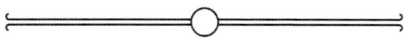

Sequoia Patterson

Summer was good to me, but I was ready to dive back into my books. It was the first day of school, and I could barely sleep the night before. I was too excited. I needed to set the vibe, so I popped my favorite tape in the cassette player—Biggie's *Ready to Die* was my "get-up-and-go" album. After finding my favorite song, I showered, dressed and tied a scarf on my head, because I never did my hair.

When I looked in the mirror, something didn't look right. "Your body's filling out, girl," I thought to myself. I had on my cute, tight red Levi's, a snug black shirt, and my 54-11s—black with a red bandana. "Nah, that hair gotta be done. The boys are checking for you more now. Get your hair right!" I said to myself. I brushed my hair up into a feathered ponytail and went on my way. The second year of high school was gonna be a breeze.

My boyfriend was a block boy. He had a little money and he kissed good. I had a beeper, a two-finger ring and snack money. What more could a girl ask for? I spent my summer running to the store and taking my little cousins to the park. Sounds boring, but those were the things I had to do to get outside.

You'd see me with a trail of kids circling the block, always on the lookout for my next "victim." I knew every hustler on the block and I wanted all of them—well, honestly, I wanted their *money*—for snacks and to get my hair done. I headed to the 17 bus that would take me straight to school. My best friend was late, as usual, so we agreed to meet in the lunchroom.

Walking into school, I passed the security booth, feeling a little nervous. My summer had also introduced me to gang life. I was never *in* a gang, but I'd learned how to spit a razor blade like a pro. Keeping a blade in your mouth was the easiest way to have a weapon on you without getting caught. I thought the security guards would stop me, but nope—I was in. Straight to the lunchroom I went, waiting on my besties. I grabbed breakfast, 'cause those English muffins and chocolate milk were everything. I found a table near the front, even though all the cool kids sat in the back. I wanted to spot my friend as soon as she walked in.

With my feet kicked up on a chair, stuffing my face, in came the coolest security guard in the school. She walked over, pushed my feet off the chair, and said, "Loosen the button on those pants—you're suffocating that baby!"

What are you talking about?" I said.

A smirk crept across her face. "You *know* what I'm talking about."

"I'm NOT pregnant!" I snapped.

Let's be clear, I was not a virgin. I even had a damn sex calendar that me and my bestie made so that I could track who I gave it to. But that got old quick, so I decided to stop checking for all the hustlers on the block. I cut my rotation down to Drugga, and we started sleeping together before my 15th birthday. In my mind, I thought we were in a relationship, even though we were never together in public. We had a signal: I'd nod to let him know we could meet, and he'd nod toward a building. That meant to meet him on the roof of that particular building. This is where all of our sex sessions took place. We never used protection, and the truth is, I never used protection with anyone I slept with.

I was able to go speak to my therapist after the conversation that I had with the security guard. She asked if I wanted to take a pregnancy test and I said yes. And sure enough it came back positive. I was so confused when I left her office I went straight to see the block boy and told him on that same roof that I think the baby was conceived on. "Who is the father?" His reaction didn't surprise me, because he knew I was sleeping with a couple of other people. The weeks ahead were so stressful. There was no conversation about what should happen to the baby. My grandmother made an appointment for me to get an abortion. My cousin took me to the clinic, but when the doctors described the procedure, I started crying and saying, "I don't want to do it." My cousin took me home, but my grandmother was still like, "Nah, you have to get rid of it," so the next person to take me to the clinic was my aunt. By that time, I was five months pregnant, and the doctor refused to perform the procedure. I had so many mixed emotions. I'd lie on my stomach to try and make myself have a miscarriage, but that didn't work. But then two minutes later, I wanted to keep my baby. My family was so upset about the pregnancy that they never spoke about it or asked how I was feeling.

Christmas was right around the corner and my stomach was huge and the baby was moving around. I made a store run for my grandmother, but as usual, I made a detour to see if I could spot Drugga hanging out. Outside, a day after a snowstorm, Drugga was with a girl whose stomach was just as big as mine. I wanted to stop and talk to him, but kept it moving. I attended my doctor visits alone, a reminder that my alleged baby father and I weren't in a relationship. All I could think about was that this man really had a girlfriend—and she was pregnant too.

As my February due date approached, I didn't know what to expect. I practiced breathing and push-ing, but I was so scared. Would I die? Could I do this? Was I strong enough? My due date came and went, no baby, no labor pains. But the day after Valentine's Day, I spent the day in excruciating pain. That night, I dreamed about monkeys. Ironically, I was imagining how my baby would look. In my dream, every time a monkey swung on the bars, I felt the urge to push. Suddenly, I woke up in a puddle.

"I must've peed the bed," I thought, clutching my stomach as the pain became unbearable.

My aunt walked in and scrunched up her face. "It stinks in here."

"I know. I just peed in the bed," I said.

She laughed, "Girl, that's not pee. Your water broke."

I didn't know what that meant, but apparently it meant the baby was coming.

My aunt called the ambulance, but the elevator in our building was broken. We lived on the tenth floor, so the paramedics carried me down the steps. Every bump and turn made the pain worse.When we reached the front door, they hit one last bump, and I started screaming. "This baby is coming out now!"

And just like that, in the ambulance, in front of my building, my first child was born with a cone-shaped head, loud cries and pale skin. I was instantly in love. On February 15th, at 7 pounds, 12 ounces, I became a mother for the first time. I was so happy. Even though my aunt wasn't happy about my pregnancy, she helped me name him KJ. At home, everyone wanted to meet my little bundle of joy. But the only person I could think about was my baby father.

About a month later, I saw Drugga in my aunt's building. As the elevator doors opened, he walked in. We rode in silence. Then, he lifted the hood of the stroller to peek at the baby, but that was it. The elevator ride felt like forever. When I got off, I cried in the hallway. I never made it to my aunt's apartment. I just rode the elevator back down and went home. Drugga never made an effort to see my child. I guess he thought I was content with being a single mom. Thankfully, I loved my baby enough for the both of us.

The next few months were easier. Summer was approaching and I was back outside, moving like I'd never left. Men wanted me even more now that I was pushing a stroller. And I was back to sleeping with Drugga. This time we were at my grandmother's house. My aunts were in Staten Island and I had free range of the house, and the living room was our fucking playground—literally. Aside from messing around with Drugga, I was back in business with some old flings and a few new ones too, and I was happy.

It was June, and I was excited to celebrate my 17th birthday. Then, I got the biggest surprise of my life—I was pregnant again. This time, I wasn't sure who fathered this baby. From my calculations, the only possible option was Drugga. Again! Having another baby by him when he wasn't taking care of the first one was crazy, especially when I knew he wasn't going to do anything different.

And his girlfriend was pregnant again too. What are the fucking odds? After two babies, you think I would've learned my lesson, but I didn't. Unfortunately, it took having three children (with two baby fathers), getting arrested and losing freedom and my kids to the system to finally realize that I was chasing something I was never gonna find with my vagina. After three long years of being homeless and fighting to get my kids out of the system, I finally knew that I needed to learn how to love myself, and I did…until I didn't again.

I AM THE CHANGE

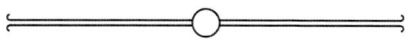

Helen "Skip" Skipper

If you've ever wondered what it's like to straddle two worlds—the one that sees "otherness" and the one where you are the expert, recognized as both a survivor and fighter—you're in for a story that's raw and unfiltered!

I've been around the block a time or two on my tricycle, and let me tell you, the criminal justice system isn't just about laws and procedures. No, it's about people. I've lived it all, from spending years cycling through incarceration to sitting at the helm of programs designed to uplift those of us who walked that walk. I have seen firsthand how a system that's supposed to serve us can trap and negate us. Let's get real for a minute: every case hides a far more complicated story than any set of numbers can ever tell.

When I first stepped into the system, I wasn't a number—I was a person with big dreams and real fears, carrying a heavy load of life's harsh baggage. I saw lives reduced to files and notes, stripped of the sordid, beautiful human experience. If I got the chance to create a system, it would be one that heals, not hurts and the first action step would be to start with listening.

This is essential because how do you understand the backstory of someone caught up in a whirlwind of unfortunate events due to unchecked mental illness and addiction without listening? I've been that person. I've had to fight every day against the idea that my painful past negates my worth. I'm not excusing my criminal behavior or the harm I've perpetrated. Still, I'm pointing out that when you understand the why, then you also understand the person behind it—a living human being.

I spent 25 years (starting at age 17) cycling through the criminal justice, mental health, homelessness and substance abuse systems. I'm heavily impacted by these many systems of oppression. All along, it should have been obvious to anyone who took one look at me that I was in desperate need of help. I suffered from an untreated serious mental illness that I was self-medicating with illicit substances. I was arrested on dozens of occasions for drug and theft offenses. And yet, at no time in this extensive period was I ever offered a meaningful chance to get connected to the treatment and services. I needed these to safely exit the criminal legal system, to treat these root causes and to recover from the decades of trauma these institutions had inflicted on me. Instead, for 25 years, I was shuffled off to the next place, only to rinse and repeat the same cycle over and over again.

It stings when someone sees you as a statistic. I've been there, every arrest and decision rendered me a faceless number. But I'm not a statistic—I'm a promising woman with a hopeful life, turning hard knocks into stepping stones for change. Growing up in a Black, marginalized community, I was no stranger to the harsh realities of being judged by the color of my skin and past mistakes. I still hear echoes of those days when every interaction with the criminal justice system felt like a reminder of my being "less than," part of the never-woulda-shoulda-coulda club. According to them, I was *never* going to be anything. I would *never* succeed. I should've been left in jail. I could *never* hope to live as a responsible citizen. Yada, yada, yada.

Newsflash: those experiences didn't break me—they built me up.

I've seen it numerous times, especially with folks caught up in drug-related charges. In many communities, addiction isn't about being weak, lazy or morally failing—it's about being starved for support, understanding and a fair chance at life. I've seen my peers judged for yesterday's poor decisions, instead of who they are today. We have been demonized for what, in a different world, would be treated as a public health issue. And that, my friends, is a slap in the face to everyone who believes in the power of second chances.

My two cents? Embrace the uniqueness that shapes each person's journey. Look past the labels and see the whole human being. The world isn't black and white—it's a jumbled, convoluted, colorful mix of experiences, pain, promise and hope. If we want our criminal justice system to be more than just a conveyor belt of punishment on the escalator to hell, we need to start treating people with respect, like members of humanity. Yeah, imagine that!

I've spent years working with people whose lives were upended by a system that treats them like numbers. I've sat with peers, listened to their raw, unfiltered stories and seen how those narratives—including my own—are full of pain, hope and grit. When I tell my story, it's about understanding that my journey, like so many of ours, is complex and full of lessons we can't ignore. If you listen closely, it opens hearts and changes minds. I'm sharing the lived reality of people written off by society, reminding everyone that behind every file number is a life worth fighting for. That's why I'm passionate about including our voices in every discussion about reform. When we let the real stories in, we start to see that our system shouldn't be about punishment alone but healing, understanding and redemption. Every arrest, setback, and cold look from someone who didn't believe in me added fuel to my fire.

Today, I'm the Vice Chair of the NYC Board of Correction and a nationally recognized leader who is a subject-matter expert in criminal justice reform. I still battle the ghosts of stigma—the constant reminder of the years I spent trapped in a system that never really wanted me to succeed. My journey, from a young woman caught in a system that never gave her a break to a published scholar and fearless advocate for lived-experience inclusion, is proof that our stories matter. They're proof that what we've been through can become the foundation of a better, fairer and more humane system that rehabilitates rather than drowns in punitiveness.

I'm not just laying bare my struggles—I'm asking a question that burns inside me: Where are all the impacted women leaders? Where are the voices that have been shunned, silenced and ignored? I've seen the data, know the numbers and I have lived the experience. I've been honored, awarded and even had the privilege of speaking at events where I represent not just my own journey but the journeys of countless others. And let me tell you, if we can break free from the chains of stigma and show up with our full, authentic selves, we can reshape this broken system from the inside out.

MY FATHER TAUGHT ME HOW TO BE A SIDE CHICK

Bridget Wilson

It was November 19, 1983, and there I was dressed in an all-white flowy gown with a veil hiding my face. Excited, but nervous, I gripped my bouquet of flowers and practiced how I'd walk down the aisle. The bridesmaids were so encouraging. "Bridget, you're the cutest flower girl we've ever seen," they said "Don't forget to toss the flower petals on the floor!"

When the music started, I walked down the aisle, my eyes focused on my dad, the man at the altar, who was ready to take his vows. He was six feet tall, with wavy hair and a beautiful yellow hue. "My daddy is so handsome," I thought to myself. As I approached, my dad's smile beamed brighter and brighter. The words he mouthed to me made my confidence grow: "You look beautiful, baby."

My dad was my world. He had my heart, and I didn't want to do anything without his approval. He spoiled me with gifts, attention and adoration. He cooked for me and we watched our favorite TV shows while sitting on the couch. And his hugs? My dad gave me energy and comfort. I felt happy in his presence. Then…he left and my world was turned upside down. I was so confused. I didn't know where he went or why he left.

I was five years old when I was forced from my home and had to live with my grandmother, my aunts and my cousins. My parents were married for two years before the divorce. During their marriage, my mother had an affair with a Panamanian king pin. She had access to everything in this man's world, including crack. Once my dad got wind of this information, life as I knew it was over.

My grandmother's home was immaculate. It had wall-to-wall carpet, coupled with the latest furniture and appliances. I had home cooked meals every night, trendy clothes and the most elaborate vacations. And I served at church as a junior usher and choir member. My new environment gave me everything I'd ever wanted, but it couldn't give me the one thing that I needed: my dad.

On my 11th birthday, my dad came to visit me. I was elated. He gave me a yellow stopwatch, which at that time was a status symbol that I could brag about and show to my friends. I expected my dad to stay and eat cake and ice cream with me. But he left, leaving me with his work phone number, in case I "wanted to talk." That birthday was bittersweet.

My grandmother was an excellent provider. But what I really needed was emotional support and one-on-one attention. This wasn't too much to ask because she gave it to my little sister, while my request for those things fell on deaf ears. This caused me to be angry, confused and resentful. I went from being a sweet, quiet church girl to a rebellious teen who lacked emotional control. So, at 13, I ran away to my father's house. During one of our conversations, he'd give me his home address and told me to "come over anytime." On the way to the bus station, I ran into my grandmother, and I rolled my eyes and walked past her. I was over her.

During that 20-minute bus ride to Roosevelt, Long Island, I felt free. Free from the lack of attention, free from the lack of mental support, free from confusion, free to be with my dad. My dad introduced me to his girlfriend who was a tall, curvy chocolate woman, who didn't say too much. To my surprise there were twin girls sitting in the living room.

"Daddy, who are these little girls"? I said.

"They are your sisters, Angela and Abigail," he replied.

All I could think was, *Damn, I'm NOT daddy's little girl anymore.* Despite this shocking surprise, I got comfortable with my new environment. I mentally prepared myself to take the bus ride from Roosevelt to Hempstead for school, but that was okay, because I was excited and ready to begin this new chapter with my dad.

My new situation lasted three days. On the third day, my dad came home from work, and I'd just finished cleaning the house, like my grandmother taught me to do. When my father told me to, "Put all the cleaning supplies away and come sit at the kitchen table." I sat down across from him. "Bridget, you have to leave my house because my girlfriend doesn't like you," he said. I have no words to express the feeling that came across my body as he uttered those words. It felt like an out of body experience. All I could do was pack my bags. A piece of my heart was permanently broken that day.

I rode the bus in silence. My 13-year old mind tried to process the information, the rejection. At home, I opened the front door with my tail between my legs. My grandmother was in the kitchen cooking, but I didn't speak to her. Quickly, I walked past her and went to my bedroom and cried. My grandmother never came to my room to console me, nor did we have a heart-to-heart talk. I never told her what happened. We went about life as usual. Thinking back, my grandmother probably knew my dad wasn't shit and waited patiently for me to return.

That day, my father's words planted a seed of pain in my heart and mind. That seed blossomed into more anger and more resentment, and I tried to cover up the pain with a series of empty relationships.

ALL BOYS, NO MEN

When I was 18, I met Sauce, a man who was ten years my senior. He was originally from Harlem, but his family moved to Hempstead when he was a teenager. Sauce was quiet, almost six-feet tall with a stocky build; and he "got money" which meant he was a drug dealer, but he also had a regular 9-to-5 job too. He wasn't like the dumb ass boys in high school who tried to get with me. He was smooth, charming and charismatic. His energy turned me on. When he approached me, I knew he was fresh out of a relationship with his children's mother, but that didn't stop me from being instantly attracted to him. Immediately, he made me feel comfortable, beautiful and worthy. He treated me like a princess. We went on dates and he bought me gifts. It didn't take long for him to rekindle his relationship with his ex, and when he did I cut him off. I liked Sauce but it wasn't love.

Later that year, I met a sexy ass man named L.A. If you can picture Omar Epps and Nas combined, that is what L.A. looked like. I will never forget our first meeting. I traveled to the Bronx to his house and when I got to his building, he stood in the doorway waiting for me. In my head I said, "Damn, if he asks for some, I'm giving it to him!" And I did. He claimed me as his girlfriend and I moved in with him. Once again, things were looking good. L.A. cooked for me, did my laundry and gave me money. I fell in love with him. L.A., who was three years older than me, had a certain swag that Sauced lacked. And L.A.'s family embraced me. We had dinners with them, which was something I'd had before, it felt like the hood version of *The Cosby Show*.

Soon, I found that L.A. lied about his age. He was one year *younger* than me. When I confronted him about it, I said: "I don't fuck with young niggas. I like older niggas and you know that." Then, I proceeded to call him a lying ass bitch. That comment enraged him. He threw me on the bed, sat on the top of my torso and punched me in the face. I managed to wiggle around to grab a small wooden bat from the nightstand. I hit him in the face with it until he got off me. Frantic, I packed my bags to leave. But he grabbed all of my designer clothes and dropped them in the motor oil that had spilled on the floor outside of our door.

I left with the clothes on my back and three outfits. Soon, I found out I was pregnant with our first daughter. But he didn't find out about her until after she was born, and we rekindled our relationship. The honeymoon was short-lived, but it was long enough to make a second baby, and the abuse started again. While I was recovering from delivering our second child, I heard him talking to someone on the phone.

"Yeah, she had the baby," L.A. said. "What are you cooking for dinner tonight? I'll be home soon."

If I had the strength to get out the bed to stab him, I would have. The woman on the other end was his girlfriend. I couldn't believe it.

"Girlfriend?!," I yelled. "How the hell do you have a girlfriend, when I'm living with you and just gave birth to your second child?"

My self esteem was crushed. I felt betrayed and broken. But I decided to give him another chance because I didn't want our daughters to grow up without their father–like I did. But they would be without him for a short while anyway. When our second daughter was two months old, L.A. was sentenced to two years in prison for a drug charge.

This gave me time to think about the choices I'd made. It was time to break free from the abuse (even if it meant my children wouldn't grow up in the same house as their father) and find peace of mind. I moved back to Hempstead, got my first apartment and started a new life. I embraced my newfound freedom to the fullest. I reunited with old friends, and started dating Rowdy, a dude from the hood. Rowdy was known for getting into all types of shit, especially robbery. When he was a kid he set the incinerator on fire and several families had to abandon their homes due to the damage. Why would I want someone like that? I saw past the crazy reputation to his "softer side," and Rowdy was sweet to me.

Rowdy introduced me to his friend Cash. While Rowdy was messing around with his ex and another girl across town, Cash and I would hang out, go to the park and play ball. We became fast friends. When Rowdy was sentenced to five years in prison, my friendship with Cash grew. Cash was an up-and-coming hustler, but later, when he assembled a team, I became his chief of staff.

We worked well together because we were both smart. We built a bond and trust with one another; and Cash became my best friend. We slept in the bed together head to foot many times and he never tried anything, and even though he was fine, I never looked at him in a romantic way. But soon, we fell in love with each other. He had my heart. But little did I know that my heart was about to take yet another beating.

Cash had beef with an uncle and nephew duo. This led to Cash getting shot. And in true ride-or-die fashion, I rushed to the hospital ready to be by his side. When I walked into the room, another girl was already there. Neither of them explained who she was. My intuition told me something was going on. But I put my feelings to the side to attend to my man's needs. At the end of the visit, Cash asked me to drive her home in his car. That was the longest ride to Brooklyn! Baby, it was a long ride. We listened to the radio in silence. But my mind was having a full-on press conference. I had so many questions with no answers. But the fear of getting my heart broken—again—kept me silent.

A few days later, I picked Cash up from the hospital. He was on crutches, so he slept on the couch instead of going upstairs to the bedroom. And I slept on the loveseat so that I could be at his beck and call, but he thought I went upstairs. That's how I caught him on the phone talking to Krissy, the girl from the hospital.

"I miss you too, baby. I'm just staying here until I get better," he said. "You think that I'd rather be here than with you"? As he uttered those words, rage took over my body. As soon as he hung up the phone, I got up off the couch, turned on the lights and said, "Surprise, motherfucker!" And I began to whip his ass with that crutch. I hit him across his head, back and chest. When I got tired of hitting him, I spit in his face and threw him down a flight of stairs and tossed all his medications and clothes behind him. I was over him.

But we ended up in this cycle of getting back together and breaking up—again and again. In the end, Cash and Krissy moved to Atlanta and bought a house and lived there with their two children. For years, he wanted us to be in a polygamous relationship. At first, I was willing to do it, just to have him in my life. I didn't want Krissy to feel like she'd won.

But in all honesty, I thought I was winning, but I wasn't. I lost my sense of self, lost my confidence, lost my sense of reasoning, and I lost my common sense when it came to Cash. After years of back and forth, I made the decision to let go and to work on me. I took a vow of celibacy, went to counseling and became focused on my spirituality.

Building Bridges

My dad has five children. I grew up in the same building with my brother and we hung out often. His mother referred to me as her daughter, and it felt good to have that connection. But as we got older, something changed and his mother interfered in our brother-sister relationship. My cousin Nicholos did an ancestry.com test and ended up connecting with another family member who turned out to be my sister, Gianna. She was born a week before my parents' wedding day, so yeah, my dad was double dicking. Giana and I met for the first time at Nicholos' wedding. We're working on creating a bond that goes beyond communicating on the Internet.

Speaking of the Internet, I found the twins on Facebook. They thought I was a cousin, which forced me to explain that I was their oldest sister and recall the three days we lived together. They were in shock. That put me in such a weird headspace. Like, what time of shit was my father on? How the fuck do they not know about me? We haven't met in person yet, but we do show each other love online. I'm praying that we'll all meet in person soon.

As far as my dad is concerned, he still treats me the same way he always has. We talk on the phone in ten-minute intervals. I go by his house, he comes and sits in my car and gives me money, kisses me on the cheek and leaves. It's always the same. But he flies out to Florida to spend quality time with Angela and Abigail, even after I asked to be included in these special trips. But he hasn't done it. For the life of me, I don't understand why he treats his first-born child this way, and honestly, I don't have the bandwidth to try to understand. I have made the conscious decision to limit contact with him. From now on I'm loving and empowering me and breaking the stigma he left me with as a "side chick."

Being a fatherless child in the hood is not for the weak. Since going to counseling and getting to the root cause of my trauma, I'm able to navigate relationships more successfully. Now, I understand who I am and what I bring to the table in a platonic or romantic relationship. I know now that I don't have to "perform" in order for a man to love and take care of me properly. I have created boundaries and a standard for how I want to be treated. I now know that sex is not a negotiating tool to gain love, but instead an expression of love.

THE LAST WORD

I'm a sucker for a good anthology, especially one that centers women. So, when Dr. Nadia Lopez invited me to participate in this project, it was an immediate "hell yes" for me. Most anthologies simply put out a call for essays, which is fine, but this one allowed me to lead writing workshops and be fully immersed in the storytelling and writing process. But the biggest (and best) perk? That was meeting the women in person at our L.I.T.T.Y Retreat and later, watching them transform during their photo shoot.

When it came time to brainstorm a title for the anthology you're holding in your hands, I kept coming back to HBO's *If These Walls Could Talk* anthology, because the movie connects the plights of three women and their abortion experiences. And while *If These Scars Could Talk* has a different subject matter, the L.I.T.T.Y writers have a common experience too. They are women doing dope things with their lives and careers—post incarceration.

The L.I.T.T.Y writers have lost so much, but they've also gained so much too: clarity, strength, resilience and a deeper understanding of who they are, the choices they made and the sacrifices it took to "rewrite" their life stories. Each story is an act of resistance and rejection of labels like "inmate," "felon" or criminal." Each author's journey is a reminder that recovery means reclaiming your voice, your dignity and your right to be seen as whole, worthy and human.

Healing is a communal act and it's one that requires the absence of judgment, so thank you for seeing these women and seeing them beyond their *wounds* to their *wisdom.*

—**Taiia Smart Young**, book coach and storytelling strategist

MEET THE AUTHORS

Cassandra Cean-Owens is a proud mother and dedicated wife known as the "Chief Compassion Officer". She is a dynamic consultant, professional speaker, and advocate with over two decades of interdisciplinary expertise as a lawyer, nurse, and organizational development leader. Drawing from her lived experience as a justice-impacted individual, Cassandra's leadership philosophy emphasizes character development, resilience, and transformation. With a deep understanding of the challenges faced by diverse and marginalized communities, she brings a uniquely empathetic and empowering perspective to every space she enters.

Chrystal Colón is a passionate dancer, fashion enthusiast, and storyteller committed to elevating voices and creating spaces of empowerment. With a background in communications and media, she combines creativity with advocacy, utilizing her passion for design and movement to express herself and build resilience. Chrystal, a devoted mother and natural visionary, dedicated to encouraging people, prioritizing education, and redefining what it means to overcome adversity with strength.

Shameeka France held the position of Project Lead at Columbia University in the City of New York from January 2022 to November 2023. Her responsibilities included assisting the director of The Center for Institutional & Social Change in guiding law students on topics related to equity, inclusion, and democracy. Prior to this role, Shameeka served as a motivational speaker for the NYC Department of Education, focusing on outreach to troubled youth in Brooklyn at Boys and Girls High School.

Jusinta Jaggassar-Ernul is a dynamic community Peer Mental Health and Substance Use Recovery Coach and Consultant, certified by New York State. With over 15 years of international and domestic leadership experience, Jusinta is also a seasoned Global Senior Program Manager, Systems Science and

Industrial Engineering Consultant, and Lean Six Sigma Master Black Belt. She brings a global perspective shaped by her experiences living and studying in Mexico, Belgium, Germany, Amsterdam, London, Paris, and Brazil. Beyond her professional endeavors, Jusinta is a dedicated mother of two beautiful children and honors them through her work. She is a committed community leader and philanthropist, passionate about creating impact through service. Based in New York, she enjoys traveling, cross-country family track events, swimming, and photography.

K. Sweetness Jennings is an African American warrior woman, poet, caregiver, change agent, cycle breaker and sojourner of truth. A Queens native, who is a recent widow and mother to two extraordinary young men who are both college graduates. She has worked as a credentialed substance abuse counselor for more than 15 years, including outpatient and inpatient detox modalities for men and women. Sweetness earned a bachelor's degree in sociology from the College of New Rochelle (in Manhattan) and a master's in professional studies from New York Theological Seminary. She is a humble servant of the Most High.

Samantha J. Lawrence is a dynamic Brooklyn native of Caribbean descent. She has transformed her life experiences—including incarceration—into a 13-year journey of advocacy and social work. Samantha is currently pursuing her LCSW and a doctorate in social work while leading nonprofit initiatives that have earned her a citation and resolution. Beyond her professional work, she finds joy in chasing waterfalls, practicing herbalism, crafting rhinestone shoes for children, designing tumblers, and indulging in a good crab boil. Samantha is the youngest in her family and is a devoted cat mom to Phaze.

Kifana Longdon-Gordon welcomed her first son into the world at the age of 16. Despite the demands of raising a child, she graduated from high school at 17. Later, Kifana earned a bachelor's degree in business administration. She firmly believes in the principle of "each one, teach one," which led her to pursue a second bachelor's degree in human services to make a positive impact on her community. Kifana was born in St. Vincent and the Grenadines but resides in Brooklyn with her husband and four sons. She is passionate about community outreach and engaging with youth to empower them at every level. Kifana is committed to creating opportunities for others to succeed.

Dr. Nadia Lopez is an award-winning educator, author, and social impact leader dedicated to transforming underserved communities through education and empowerment. As the founding principal of Mott Hall Bridges Academy in Brownsville, Brooklyn, her work garnered national attention through Humans of New York, leading to a $1.4 million GoFundMe campaign and a meeting with President Barack Obama. Her TED Talk, *Why Open a School? To Close a Prison*, highlights her mission to disrupt the school-to-prison pipeline and has inspired audiences globally. Dr. Lopez has received numerous honors, including the Black Girls Rock! Change Agent Award, LinkedIn Top Voice in Education, and recognition as a finalist for the Global Teacher Prize. She currently empowers justice-involved women through education and civic engagement, working to dismantle systemic barriers within the criminal justice system. Dr. Lopez is also the author of *The Bridge to Brilliance*, and a sought-after speaker on education reform and social justice.

Penelope Martin, known as Penny to her friends and family, is originally from Brooklyn, New York, but currently resides in Westchester County. She works full-time for an organization that provides higher education to incarcerated individuals. During her own incarceration, she earned both her associate and bachelor's degrees through Hudson Link for Higher Education in Prison. Penelope is a mother and grandmother who is now attending Yeshiva University, where she is pursuing a master's degree in social work.

Turquoise Juanita Martin is a proud Harlem native, visionary leader, and advocate who transforms adversity into empowerment. Overcoming foster care, sex trafficking, addiction, sex work, and generational trauma, Turquoise channels her resilience and creativity into healing, the arts, and inspiring others. She pairs her education with urban savvy to transmute her lived experience into lived expertise, contributing to her community through her spiritual empowerment business, Doza Kingdom. Turquoise loves being a mom to her son, Elisha, and her cat, Prosper.

Sequoia Patterson is a dedicated community activist, mother of five, and passionate advocate for gun violence prevention. With a deep commitment to social justice, she has worked in various roles but finds the greatest fulfillment in her current position as a Hospital Responder Supervisor at a nonprofit organization, where she has served for three years. Sequoia holds multiple certifications that enhance her ability to serve her community. Her unwavering dedication has been recognized by the Mayor's Office, which awarded her a Certificate of Recognition for her impactful work. Beyond her professional achievements, Sequoia is committed to uplifting youth affected by the justice system. She is actively developing a program aimed at providing mentorship, resources, and guidance to help them navigate challenges and create brighter futures.

Helen "Skip" Skipper has led in peer support workforce development since her final release from incarceration in 2007. In 2022, she became Executive Director of the NYC Justice Peer Initiative. A nationally recognized expert, Skip advocates for the inclusion of lived experiences and designs justice-involved support programs. She consults with the NYPD, Urban Institute, and other organizations. She is currently a criminology master's candidate (on track for a PhD) and a published academic author. Skip serves as the Vice Chair of the NYC Board of Correction and holds positions on several criminal justice reform agency boards.

Taiia Smart Young is a book coach, writing consultant and story strategist. She teaches coaches, consultants, speakers and entrepreneurs how to use their expertise and experiences to write and publish brand-building books and stories that make bank. As an on-camera host and interviewer, Taiia has been in conversation with Michelle Obama, Mary J. Blige. Nas, 50, Tabitha Brown, La La Anthony and more. Her work has appeared in *ESSENCE*, *Latina*, Refinery29.com, TIDAL, Verizon.com and *The New York Times*.

Bridget Wilson is a native of Hempstead, New York. She is a mother of two adult children and a grandmother to one. She has survived domestic violence, incarceration, abandonment, and homelessness to become an author, teacher, real estate agent, and investor. Bridget's goal is to inspire women who feel hopeless through her writing and business ventures. One of her favorite roles is that of a baker, and she is known for her famous strawberry crunch cupcakes.

College &
Community
Fellowship

About the Organization:

The College and Community Fellowship (CCF) is dedicated to supporting women impacted by incarceration through the transformative power of education and access. With a focus on helping women achieve their educational and career goals through mentorship, advocacy, and skill development, CCF provides access to resources that empower participants to navigate the complexities of higher education and reintegration into society, ultimately fostering personal growth and community leadership.

www.collegeandcommunity.org

www.ingramcontent.com/pod-product-compliance
Lightning Source LLC
Chambersburg PA
CBRC090838120626
46551CB00008B/696